# KINGFISHER DAYS

## MARY SHEEPSHANKS

WITHDRAWN FROM THE POETRY LIBRARY

**Fighting Cock Press**

First published by Fighting Cock Press 1998
This edition reprinted 2004

**Fighting Cock Press**

**Fighting Cock Press:**
45 Middlethorpe Drive
York
YO24 1NA

Editor: Pauline Kirk
Consultant: Mabel Ferrett

Printed by Peepal Tree Press
Cover Design by Graham Rust
Original Fighting Cock Logo by Stanley Chapman

ISBN  0 906744 17 2

**Acknowledgements are due to the following:**

**Journals**
*Acumen, Aireings, The Countryman, Camphill Correspondence, Farmers Weekly, The Field, Pennine Platform, Poetry Now, Yorkshire Journal*

**Anthologies**
*Still More Christmas Crackers 1990 – 2000*
Commonplace selections by John Julius Norwich
*Pennine Poets' Chapbook*
Edited by Mabel Ferrett and Pauline Kirk
*Pennine Tracks*
Edited by Clare Chapman

*Lullaby* has been set to music by Paul Dutton
*No Response* has been set to music by Caroline McCausland

*Fighting Cock Press* and the author gratefully acknowledge permission from *Penguin Books* to include three poems which first appeared in *The Bird of my Loving* by Mary Sheepshanks.

**Also by Mary Sheepshanks**

**Fiction**
*A Price for Everything*
*Facing the Music*
*Picking up the Pieces*
*Off-Balance*
*The Venetian House* (writing as Mary Nickson)

**Non Fiction**
*The Bird of my Loving*
(A personal response to loss and grief)

**Poetry**
*Patterns in the Dark*
*Thinning Grapes*
*Dancing Blues to Skylarks*

**This book is dedicated
to my grandchildren, with love and gratitude.**

# Contents

## Dragons

Some Dragons
fan such fierce furnaces
they can forge poetry
and progeny simultaneously.

My fires were not
strong enough for that
though I have puffed out
both in my time;

poems are
my children now
– but my children are
still my best poems.

## Kingfisher Days

An electric flash of unexplained delight
– a kingfisher moment – streaked across my day,
like blue-green rockets torched on bonfire night.
Where did it come from? Why? I cannot say.

When Turner dreamed of painting storms at sea
or mixed his palette for The Téméraire
did he recall a Yorkshire memory
of walking by the Washburn valley, where

he must have seen a feathered shaft of light
explode above dark waters, felt the thrill
of unexpected colour flood his sight,
and held his breath, heart-stopped, on heathered hill?

Kingfisher days grow scarce. I watch and wait:
send me one more – before it is too late.

## Kippers and Cow Parsley
(*In memory of my mother*)

Talking of kippers and cow parsley
I thought immediately of you.

Both would be luxuries if they were rare:
the one so highly flavoured,
pungent, strong
– caviar for unpretentious homes –
the other hedgerow lace
of beautiful simplicity,
– quite without artifice.

We never had to guess
your stream of thought:
no muddy waters, stagnant pools or tributaries,
your little burn flowed clear and bright
straight down a narrow channel;
its force and energy
could well have turned a mill-wheel
and ground corn – good wholemeal flour
for family consumption –
but not to be gobbled up
by stray lame ducks.

Children you loved, and birds,
looked not unlike
a small pied flycatcher yourself
– so darting and alert –
watchful to snatch at any chance
for nurturing your chicks.

I borrowed your car once
and moved the driving mirrors
"Don't worry, darling, that's alright,"
you said, "I never use them anyway."
Not for you the backward glance,
careful avoidance of collision
or keeping to the inside lane.

You were never much inclined
to dwell on shelf-life:
no silly nonsense about sell-by dates
or "best before..."
at ninety you applied for a new Railcard
answering "Hobbies and Interests?"
with a single word:
LIVING you wrote, heavily underlined.

You kept no airs and graces
in your wardrobe, and could be sharp
with flashy dressers rash enough
to wear them in your presence
– yet now my post brings tributes to surprise you:
"She was a great lady" and
"We shall not see the like of her again"

Life will be very dull without you, Mum,
but thank you for those generous years
of biased love.

## Love Song

When I was young I hoped to find
my other half – a perfect mate –
to fire my heart and share the walk
that leads up to the Exit Gate.

Then I grew up – and proud and blind
thought every man had feet of clay
– unless perfection came my way
I swore I'd lock my heart away.

I was so blinkered – did not guess
that thorns and thickets hid a rose
– and foolish too, for wisdom knows
love can be true that slowly grows.

I walked and searched but did not sense
you there beside me on my climb,
and while I scanned the distant heights
your love was with me all the time.

I've learnt that love is made, not found:
hammered and honed and carved with care.
Your heart has taught me truth – and now
I've unlocked mine for you to share.

## This Cold Freedom

Is this how long-term captives
feel on their release
– afraid of open space?

I chose to stay with you
– you who were kept a prisoner
in your body for so long –
yet often, sharing your life,
it was difficult
to keep the pilot light
of mine still burning.

Though I could not regret
the choice I made,
yet sometimes I still longed
to gasp a wilder air,
sing a more carefree song.

But now that you are gone
I am afraid
– such icy fingers squeeze my lungs
I cannot breathe for them.

This freedom is so cold
– so very cold.

## Dark Wind

I watched three mallard
ride a stallion wind, and go
careering up the dark November sky
with surging grace.

I envied them
and wished that I
could rise at such a pace
above my own black gusts of loneliness.

I wished that I could fly to you again
– to have you hold my hand
and touch my face,
your laughter blend with mine
as once it did
before a shroud of pain and illness
cloaked your light.

I long to feel
your presence blowing through
the echoing space
your loss has left in me.

I know I must release you
to explore eternity
– not clutch and cling –
but all the same
I fling my anguish on the storm
and shout your name aloud
to call you back,
searching the spaces in-between
relentless clouds
for messages.

My cry is sucked up by the gale
and swallowed whole
– no flashing button
signals a reply

– I cannot find
an answering machine.


**Poplar**
(*Populus Alba Richardii*)


Green, gold and silver I see
blowing a melody through my tree:
the leaves play an airy waltz for me
rippled on strings of mystery.

Descants of silver, green and gold
blow colours of song as the tune unfolds;
every laughing leaf is a note set free
to swing in the wind of eternity.

Each leaf of gold and silver-green
is starlight heard and harmony seen;
the trunk is one but the colours are three
that spring from the root of my trinity tree.

## Sternbergias
*(In memory of Harry Ward)*

Glass in the greenhouse
is broken now,
paint is peeling
and woodwork frayed:
no order, no ripeness left to show
how once voluptuous peach trees grew
stretching espalier branches wide,
each questing shoot so perfectly tied.

Today only ghosts
of nectarines grow
in this cobweb palace of phantom fruit:
cold winds can blow
through an unlatched door,
and arrogant frost swaggers in at will,
for all has decayed
since the gardener died
– and I stand and gaze at a wreck,
dismayed.

Then into this chill
of grey despair
a yellow rustle stirs the air
and I strain my ears
to catch the sound:
and there in a corner I turn to see
a choir of postulants taking vows,
making a promise of autumn hope
– Sternbergias dressed
in habits of gold.

I listen enthraled to their top Cs' sound,
and as these spears of sunlight thrust
up through the cold October ground
I find that the sad grey ghosts
have flown.

And I know that I too must make a vow
– oh not to forget the loved and gone –
but to face the change
of the feared unknown.


## Sonnet for Octavia

If you wear foxglove bells on all your toes
and drift a haze of harebells round your head,
the wind may come and tell you where it goes
and sing you private cradlesongs in bed.

When you hold conch shells tight against your ear
they whisper silver secrets of the seas:
then hold your breath, count ten, and you might hear
a school of mermaids peddling melodies.

Clip on imagination's rainbow wings
and find and climb a magic dreaming-tree;
then go and skip and wish in fairy rings
and you will be amazed at what you see –

– provided you walk tiptoe, do not shout,
and keep those interfering grown-ups out.

## Muse

Sometimes a bird
comes to perch on my shoulder.

It sings of stars and strangeness
rainbows on snow,
and the stream
which kicks its heals up
in the valley
which I know lies waiting for me
beyond the fold in the hills.

I long for my visitor to stay;
but this is a wild bird
who bubbles invitations
to the open sky:
if I put birdlime out
it might take fright and fly,
or stick to it
– and die.

I shake lest it should not return.
It carries off my sunshine
in its beak: mists rise
and shadows change to monsters;
day becomes night.

Ah, but it's worth
trembling in the cold insistent silence
clutching at terror's bony hand,
and waiting in the dark –
just for the moment
when I first hear wings
and my singing bird flies back
to sit on my shoulder
– and whistle music in my ear.


## October Song

There are swords in the air
and trees are singing
as southwards the sun-loving
swallows are winging.

Dressed like the autumn
a robin is calling;
jewels of amber
and topaz are falling.

A wind labelled "winter"
while summer still lingers
caresses our faces
with icicle fingers,

lending us briefly
a physical rapture
of sun-softened sharpness
too fleeting to capture.

## The Bramble Route
(*A Villanelle*)

I got beguiled by frozen blackberries:
they shone so lusciously from plastic trays;
no tattered clothes, no bleeding heart or knees.

The flavour's bland: why fall for charms like these
yet ache for sharper taste and wilder ways?
I got beguiled by frozen blackberries.

This cultivated fruit in my deep freeze
took me to superstores, by motorways –
no ripped up jeans, no bleeding heart or knees.

There cash-tills rang – not oreads in trees
to sing me madrigals of mountain days.
I got beguiled by frozen blackberries!

Synthetic sweetness, neatly-packaged ease
sang blandishments from marketing displays:
"guaranteed not to scratch the heart or knees".

Next time: a bramble route through scrub and screes,
a daring scramble – love's uncharted maze –
and I'll resist the frozen blackberries
to take a risk with clothes and heart and knees.

## Starting Again
(*To Freddie*)

Watching Freddie
making castles
with his wooden bricks
I envy the optimism
with which
he bashes down old buildings:
no clinging to the past;
no whingeing; no regrets.

He gets on with it – fast.

"Let's make a better one now."
he says, scattering ruins
with a cheerful swipe –
already contemplating fresh designs
– ripe for a change.

"The next house will have a
tall, tall tower,
and the people inside
will see for miles"
says Freddie.
"Through their new windows
they'll see out to
                ... forever."
And he hums and smiles
as he piles up fallen bricks:

facing the future
– starting again.

15

## Dark at the Roots

My spirits have gone
dark at the roots.

I could take drastic action:
put on a plastic cape
and plunge
the whole lot in peroxide;
but that will deceive no one
– least of all myself –
and would give my moods
a uniform appearance
which would look
unnatural.

Perhaps I need some flashes?

Should I take my spirits to a salon
– have a few strands
coated in blue gunge,
wrapped carefully in foil
(in order to protect their brittle ends)
then cooked under a dryer?

If I had more highlights
– which can be quite becoming –
perhaps I could, once again,
face my own reflection
in the mirror?

My spirits
have always been streaky
– I've learnt to live with that –
but I don't want
to have to hide them under a hat
for the rest of my life
because, suddenly,
they have all become

too dark at the roots.




## Wearing Green

The wind is wearing green today
to shimmy through the beech trees,
breaking a two-four rhythm up
– shaking with ragtime gladness:

it kicks its heels high in the spring
and Charlestons through the leaves of May.

Dance in my heart again, green wind,
to blow the pain of loss away
and syncopate my sadness.

## All We Can Do
*(For Robert and Rosie, in memory of Laura)*

No words can comfort:
all we can do
is share your north-face
route with you.

No-one can take
your pain away
or cut bereavement's
journey short.
Perhaps you would
not want them to
– your grief is all
that's left to you
of one, so loved,
who could not stay.

All we can do
is walk with you,
and try to match
our steps to yours.
Friends do not need
acknowledgement:
don't waste your strength
to make response
– just keep on walking
day by day.

But let us share
that cold road too
– to walk a little
way with you.

## House of Questions
*(For Yorkshire artist Kitty North)*

A plume of inspiration
smokes above the house:
creative sparks have burst to flame
– for fires burn fiercely
in this grate.

The track in front is wide
and very straight;
but does it lead
to somewhere out of sight
– or back inside ?

A small red figure stands,
upon the path, bones
hunched against distractions,
coat billowing with
unpainted brush-strokes.

Perhaps she's off
over the moor
to snare elusive light on canvas;
and capture layers of air
in swirls of oils?
To shout to the wind,
out-race the clouds
and search for hidden meaning
in stone walls?

Crowded images obscure a view:
this sky is wide; this landscape bare.
What is the implication
of the things left out?

19

## Mrs Ethel Richardson

Raw hands, wind-chapped
her knuckles swollen up like ginger roots,
she wields four needles with a dextrous certainty.

If she so chose
she could devour the camera with her gaze
and still keep knitting:
she knows the pattern is engraved
inside her bones
like Calais on Queen Mary Tudor's heart.

Graceful as seals at sea,
her lumpy fingers fly; the sweater grows:
wool, water-resistant as an oil-slicked gull
translates to future warmth for men in boats;
she works with understated love and skill
at complicated, zigzag ribbed designs
– child's play to her.

She fights the elements, but cannot win
and knows a thing or three of life and death:
she can lay out a corpse without a blench,
but grieves one body not recovered
from the sea.

She charts her history in cable-stitch:
if there are slips – invisible to us –
she knows which row they're on:
that baby lost, the son gone overseas;
harsh battering from gales, and blows received
from flailing husband after closing time
– that man who now sits prisoned in a chair
felled by a different kind of stroke,
while she turns yarn to pence
to buy him beer.

Her face has been mapped out
by prize photography,
– scale showing every detail -
capturing salty pride and wide humanity,
acceptance of old age –
it's not from fear that she looks down
nor can the camera follow where her gaze is set.

Her fingers fly – but years fly faster yet:
with powerful private lens
she views her past.


*(This poem was triggered by David Morgan Rees' 1998
photographic exhibition of Traditional Yorkshire Craftspeople.
Ethel Richardson of Old Whitby was a "gansey" knitter – but
her story is from my imagination)*

*(To James – and all other children like him)*

**Sometimes...**

you leave the door ajar
that leads inside your mind,
but often you lock us out –
shut yourself in
with snakes and dinosaurs
and turn the key.

Sometimes
we can see you
looking out longingly
– your nose pressed
to a smoked glass window.

We fling our doors and windows wide
and put out saucers of milk
to tempt you in,
but our rooms stifle you
with soft furnishings:
scatter-cushions of kisses and questions
are traps to trip you up
and you turn your face away and run
from eye contact –
which hangs on walls
and threatens you

Still, I think you like to get
our invitations
– so long as we never put
RSVP.

But sometimes
– just sometimes –
before the nosy, intrusive sun gets up
to blare its searchlight into your secrets,
we meet on neutral ground
and dance together, barefoot,
while I try to synchronise
my steps to your wild music.

## Lullaby

A silken fringe of lashes
lies upon your cheek.
Your head rests heavy on my arm,
your drowsy fingers seek
love's reassurance from my hand:
you sleep.
Oh keep in sleep serenity supreme
and may your dream,
safe in the silver circle of our love,
be free from harm.
God grant that no-one breaks
the rainbow bubble of your innocence
when you awake...

... when you awake.

## Mr Moon
(*For Will and Alice*)

"I come into your bed, now"
she announces firmly,
standing no nonsense from me.

She smells of dew and daisies;
looks fresh as a first-used metaphor.
She limpets round me
inserts her thumb in mouth,
clamping it tightly as a champagne cork,
and then lies still
– but not for long.

Ideas bubble
and the cork pops out again.
"Where is your watch?
I need to put it round my leg."
"Don't squirm" I beg.
"I must. I am a wiggly worm."
We chat: she, snug in tights and vest
under the fine white nightie
that her mother wore
some thirty years before;
I, not at my best
on feather-frosted dawns at five o'clock
– but she has warmed my widow's heart
and feet.

I ask if soon
she might return to her own cot?
She says not.

We gaze in admiration at the moon
which beams white magic round my walls.
"Where has the moon gone now?" she asks.
I suggest it may have gone behind a cloud.
Just as I think she's nodding off,
she ask the inevitable "Why?"

"Open your eyes" she says, prodding
my eyelids with her thumb,
forcing them open, leaving my vision blurred,
my eyeballs numb.
"I know why Mr Moon has gone away"
– she is scornful of my ignorance –
"He's gone behind the clouds to get a baby."

Later, when cautious winter sun
wavers its welcome, but less fascinating, beams
she tells me
with the nonchalance of one accustomed
to such every day events:
"There are a lot of new moons now
and Mr Moon looks after all the babies."

Mr Moon's a modern dad it seems.

## The White Peahen

She arrived in May
        – no explanation, no warning –
exciting and unexpected as the Muse,
she looked quite unconcerned:
any astonishment was on my face.
I did not dare to hope
that she would stay.

She sauntered round my garden
like Royalty on a visit to a Council house,
friendly and gracious, yes,
but not precisely tame.
She often sun-bathed in my cabbage patch
– but just to stop me taking her for granted
wore her tiara always, night and day.
She kept her distance, so I did the same.
It would have come as no surprise
to find her toe-nails painted scarlet
and kohl upon her eyes.

After a month I hoped she might remain
but, like the Muse so often does,
she disappeared
– with just as little warning as she came.

I feared a fox and searched for her in vain.
Now I've had news of her:
she's moved to grander neighbours
up the hill and nested there
– produced three eggs.

26

No doubt she'll hatch them into poems soon
but, oh, how much I wish
she'd stayed and laid them here
– and they were mine!

## Wrongways Flowing

I read the signpost in the USA:
"To Wrongways-Flowing-River Farm" it said.
Immediately you lurched inside my head:
is there a lonely island there like you?
Do waters swirl and churn around
a secret centre, dark and tree-shadowed,
where the twisting currents go
hurling themselves against
their own strong force?

I wondered if this stretch of river,
– like a wrongways-running-mind –
has private places unexplored by us,
where whirlpools and a frightening undertow
can bubble monsters up and down
and spew them out, or suck them in again,
until they drown?

And does this struggling water ever find
its own way out
to join the mainstream flow?

## The Red Pedal Car

Little boy, little boy,
blue-eyed and fair
what are you doing alone so late?
Why do you sit in a red pedal car
a mile from the village and Council Estate?
Why do you stay on the crown of the road
at nine o'clock on a summer night
– and why is there nobody else in sight?

I stop my car
but you do not move
or pedal away to the grassy edge;
I toot my horn and smile and wave
– no rescuer darts
from the hawthorn hedge
to pick you up and move your toy.
You stay right there, alone on the road
at nine o'clock on a summer night
and there isn't a house or a soul in sight.

Little blue-eyed boy
with fine blond hair,
I drive so cautiously, carefully by
you in the road in your pedal car
– but I quickly think
that I ought to say: "Where is your Mum?
Have you lost your way?"
For somebody else might come driving past
and they might be driving
much too fast.

So I stop again and run swiftly back
at nine o'clock on this hot June night
– shadows are long in the evening light,
Cow Parsley billowing shrouds of white

– but the child has vanished, the road is blank
and there isn't a pedal car in sight.


## Hospital Days...

... are grey caterpillars
humping cautiously along,
feet suctioned to
precarious stalks of grass;

if they hang on
they might change into butterflies
and wing away;
but they may
– at any moment –
get eaten
by a hungry bird

– and disappear.

## With Care

Children hang-glide
through unexpected air;

hear secrets singing in the wind,
blow precious seconds
out of dandelion clocks
and share a dawn delight
with crowing cocks and morning bells;
wonder at fairy stories
told by shells...

but
   dread the rattling bones
that clatter under beds
at dead of night.

They crane
from open windows
turning all preconceptions
on their heads
and squeezing standard answers
inside out.

They see through soft
but powerful contact lenses
and should be clearly labelled:

'*Perishable Goods*'.

## Wild Life

Secrets
live in woods
at the back of the mind:

hopes
hide in loamy corners
burrow under roots
of flowering trees
– dive underground
if they hear footsteps.

You might have to watch
all night
to see aspirations
creep into a clearing
and dance under a full moon

– they are afraid of cameras.

Fears are furtive too
but they do not dance:
they lurk in brambles

waiting to pounce.

31

## Millennium Nativity

In the year 2000
angels did not materialize:
they sent the tidings by fax.

Joseph was made reduntant:
single parenthood's acceptable now,
and this time Mary didn't need
the Holy Ghost to come upon her,
(there's IVF by DNA),
though she received counselling
– of course.

Social Workers took the baby away:
the child might be at risk from BSE
– conditions were unhygienic
and animals are not permitted
near the birthing pool.
Anyway, the stable
had been condemned by Planning years ago.
The preservation lobby
had a try at saving it:
they hired a protest gang
who sat on the roof and shot the innkeeper
– but it didn't solve the problem.

The case has been referred to Brussels,
Geneva and The White House,
and is still under discussion.
Naturally. These things take time.
The baby may be grown up
before any conclusion is reached,
but Mary can always apply for compensation
– later.

The Shepherds read about it
in *The Star* the next day.
(Shepherds don't do the night shift now.)
As for the Magi –
well they got it on the Internet,
though astrology's still popular
and there's a help-line you can ring.

I'm afraid the story's end may be the same:
crucifixion's out of fashion,
but there are other ways.
Persons have not changed;
they're more knowledgeable, certainly,
but no wiser. No wiser at all.

It was all more credible second time round
– but I prefer the first,
less believable, version
before mystery got sanitised.
Yes, a cold coming they had of it
– again –
in two thousand AD.

## Death of a Craftsman

*(In memory of Harry Pennington)*

Let him go easily,
the old man,
slide smoothly
from the launch-pad into death.
He who so loved
to make and to maintain
has finished now
with his hard-worn and battered frame.

He lost three fingers once
– they were expendable he said:
his other hand became
more skilful for the loss.
He stood, wind-proofed,
against life's buffeting –
indigenous as oak and ash and thorn.

To watch him carve a chair,
mend clocks or paint a room
was to feel all the rhymes and metres
flowing right.
His tools were inspiration,
in his hands they sang invention.

Let him go starwards fast,
his spacecraft spirit
fired by the rocket of his finished life:
the motor has burned out
and can be jettisoned
at last.

Let him go easily.

## Tightrope

A thin wire
stretches between faith and doubt.

I walk its length
with cautious, flexing feet
using my toes to grip,
– my arms spread wide
on either side to balance me,
dreading the disconcerting
dip and sway,
a sudden treacherous trip.

Incomprehensible,
the river roars below
with swirling whirlpools
rocks and waterfalls
– and hungry undertow.

Do not look down

but keep eyes trained
upon a pinpoint star
of flickering hope,
to edge a way
across this frayed,
precarious bridge of mystery.

Is there a safety net
if I should slip?

## April 1993

Today is a robin's nest day,
softly warm and lined with expectations:
a day to shelter delicate eggs of hope.

Yesterday daffodils made obeisance
to placate the spite of hail storms
but this morning they stand up
and sing alleluias.

Today my sticky buds of optimism
burst to leaf; trees sprout with songs
and all the air is yellow with rejoicing:
today I can believe that eggs will hatch

– but then I do not live in Bosnia.

Shells have no nurturing connotations there
where nests are daily stripped apart
and wrecked, and fragile hopes
get stamped into the ground
and smashed under the cruel heel
of shameful deeds.

When will the weather change in Bosnia?

## Dunblane
*13 March 1996*

Dandelion clocks are ticking,
ticking, ticking.

Hours have run out
and the lives of little children
are blown away
by a burst of vicious puffs
as the clock strikes
– sixteen.

Their years, so light and small,
float on the wind now
carried by a wanton breath
exhaled in madness

but the echo of clocks
that stopped that day
will go on sounding

always

ticking, ticking, ticking.

## Big Issue

Hello Mummy? Baby, Mummy - Baby.
Hello, hello Mummy? Baby – Baksheesh?
Mummy? – Rupees, Dollars
Chocolate, Pens, Rupees – Mummy?

Outside Marks and Spencer
in a different continent
robuster voices challenge me to
"Read The Big Issue".
Here the chant is but a reed-thin whisper,
a dusty mutter
of contaminated air breathed in and out
through lungs encased in toast-racks.
This is Calcutta.

Children with neon smiles
skitter on bent mosquito legs;
hands, which settle briefly on our arms,
sometimes get brushed away like flies.
A bundle of discarded bones
outside the Temple – dies.

We must be careful where we walk:
we might step on a body in the gutter,
slip on the garbage,
tread upon a head amongst the squalor
and soil our tourists' shoes
– defile our bus.
We didn't come on holiday to look at this!
Surely – it's too much to expect of us?

We cleanse our fingers
with pre-packed sterile Antiseptic Wipes
till no germs linger
– but I cannot wipe the whispers
from inside my head:

Hello Mummy? Baby, Mummy – Baby.
Hello, hello Mummy? Baby – Baksheesh?
Mummy? – Rupees, Dollars
Chocolate, Pens, Rupees Mummy?

Baby Baby Baby.


**Checklist for Christmas**

Hark the Herald Santa sings:
"Jingle bells and Angels' wings";
loaded trolleys – shop till dropping –
crackers pulled and land-mines popping.

Conscience-cheque to aid the starving,
– brandy butter, start the carving –
peace on Earth, goodwill to men,
stockpile with new bombs again.

Lock the doors to any stranger,
dust the Christchild, gild the manger;
turn off news of Christmas crisis
– welfare hand-outs put up prices.

Sing a carol, raise a cheer,
Christmas comes but once a year.
What a silent holy night
– with the homeless out of sight.

## Between the Roots and Branches

"I should like to lie,"
the stranger said to me
"Beside a Jesuit, beneath an olive tree
– not in a carnal sense you understand –
no, this experience would be
a journey of experimental minds
in order to explore – a mystery. "

"What if the monk
should bring his pocket map,"
I asked, "a rambler's guide
marking restricted paths he must not take
– perhaps with preconceptions
marked upon each page?"

"Oh no," he answered
"We would both be free to stray
into the densest jungle of surmise;
to wander off alone upon our way
– then meet again,
discuss discoveries
and share surprise."

Goat's cheese; a rough red wine;
and crusty bread, devoured
with knotty arguments:
ideas spread out across Ionian sea
– or dreams, with words as wings,
floating like bells
above the vine-draped hills of Tuscany;
olives and grapes and theories,
all pressed dry.

I visualize these searchers
in their grove –
lazily stretched above arthritic roots
(which clutch at earth
with fierce determined grasp)
but staring up through silver leaves
which strive to place
tentative fingers on a question mark of sky.

And if they fail to find
a far star's window to eternity
in their discourse, at least
they'll have the right to say
to God – if such there be –

"We did our best to understand
the inexplicable – we had a try."

## Bluebells

It's their independence
I admire.

Bluebells
fend for themselves:
refusing to be part
of Flower Arrangers'
snooty art; don't bend
to other people's expectations:
they may be romantic
..... but they're not sycophantic,

Bluebells
would rather go on strike
and droop – wilfully wilting –
than be crammed
in uncongenial jam-jar groups:
they form their own
impromptu dancing troupes.
Bluebells are not
politically correct:
they don't *pretend.*

Bluebells
run, barefooted, under wild-wood trees,
blow honeyed music
through green bracken fronds
and paint May mornings purple
with their laughter
– but are not afraid
to cry in public if the day is wet.

Bluebells may be spontaneous
but they're not extraneous
..... yet.

## Moorland Song
*(For David, with love)*

Wind in the heather sings me a song
of mountains and moorland where freedom is strong
– where mists round the fir-trees drape curtains of sleep
and tear-stained with water, rock-faces weep.

Breeze in the bracken murmurs a rhyme
of city-free spaces un-cloistered as time
where chimes from the harebells wild honey-bees ring,
and crooning and droning, a cradle-song sing.

Pipits are piping: they flute me a chant
of cloud patterned hill tops with sunlight aslant
on weathered grey boulders where lichens have grown
a rusty green tracery printed on stone.

The wind and the wildness tell me a tale
to heal me and help me if courage should fail;
Oh blessing of beauty – my heart must belong
where the wind in the heather blows me a song.

## No Response?
(*A Koan*)

*What is the sound of one hand clapping?*

A skylark climbing blue ladders of song
to paint notes on the air, which though clear and strong
are drowned by the sound of a cash-till's ring?

*What is the sound of one hand clapping?*

No-one to listen when loneliness shrieks;
laughter hidden and doors kept locked;
cries of a baby whom nobody rocks?

*What is the sound of one hand clapping?*

Waves of terror which shiver and slap
on a crumbling shore as a new void gapes;
screams, unanswered, as climbers slip?

*What is the sound of one hand clapping?*

Stars of uncertainty, whispering, hissing:
search and listen - but keep on guessing
who wields that arm that has one hand missing?


*A Koan, in Zen Buddhism, is a riddle on which to meditate,
not to find an answer – since there can be no logical solution
– but to ponder on what the question may be asking us to
think about.*

44

## Lord of the Shelves

After the removal team have left
I unpack china, unwrap glass,
force ornaments and books
to have fresh neighbours,
make my possessions move
try new situations
– accept change.

They have no choice in the matter:
I am Lord of the Shelves.

But the packing case labelled
"Memories" I dare not touch;
all items here are linked
– they might not come out singly.

If I release them will they riot,
upset the new order,
refuse to go back in?

Memories have lives of their own.